ADVANCE PRAISE

"Down-to-earth, practical advice from a coach who knows her stuff. Following Maureen's steps toward self-awareness turns your divorce into a window for clarity and growth while you set limits and stay true to yourself. I recommend it to all my clients as a supportive guidebook for divorce and for negotiating contentious boundaries."

– Trish Ring, Ph.D.

Executive Coach, www.TrishRing.com

"This book is like a breath of fresh air not only for my clients but also for therapists alike. It beautifully addresses the impossible dilemma of powerlessness that single parents too often experience as the courts get bogged down and the exes uses lies, court documents and children to their own advantage. Maureen Doyle comes forward with real tools and ideas to help! This is a gift to the therapeutic world!"

– Susan Austin-Crumpton

Founder and Executive Director of The Estuary, Inc.

"This is one powerful book filled with practical advice, simple tools, and a fresh perspective on co-parenting in difficult situations. Even more than that, the title could be changed to represent any life challenge and this sage advice would support someone through it. Maureen's conversational, extremely honest, and compassionate writing style offers the reader an honest, thought provoking and highly relatable handbook to guide a single mom through rough waters into a calm horizon. This book is a must for all single parenting mothers no matter what their situation is."

– Connie Cruthirds

Writer, Master Life Coach, and Coordinator of Adam's Army to help St. Jude Children's Research Hospital

D0465399

"Few books truly can take your breath away with their insight and guide you with their unique perspective. *When Your Ex Doesn't Follow The Rules* is simply that. With her evident personal experience in the co-parenting and divorce recovery field along with her knowledge as a coach, Maureen Doyle effortlessly takes a recovering divorcee from struggling to confident and self-assured. She delivers this with understanding of not only what you are going through, but explains how you can do this with compassion and positivity. Stop reading this and go read her book – immediately!"

– Susan C. Foster

Master Coach & Author of It's Not Rocket Science: Leading, Inspiring, and Motivating Your Team To Be Their Best

"What a wonderful gift to those who are going through such a horrible experience. In my therapy practice, I have counseled many women trying to make sense of life when their ex creates constant chaos. Maureen gives examples that are exact replicas of what my clients are experiencing. I am grateful that Maureen was so courageous in sharing her own story. Just knowing that you aren't the only one going through this can help you feel less "crazy."

I especially encourage readers to take to heart what she teaches about how your body can be your radar in determining how to make decisions. Your body can remember things your brain cannot. This book is a must read for those in the early stages of divorce and healing. Go ahead and read it now to save yourself a lot of heartache!"

– Jenny Emerson

Licensed Marriage and Family Therapist

"Applicable to not only those who have experienced the trauma and drama of divorce, but also for those who are simply trying to deal with difficult people or situations, *When Your Ex Doesn't Follow The Rules* is full of sage advice and actionable steps that make for a more fulfilling life and healthier relationships. This book provides a heaping dose of inspiration and hope for reconnecting to your authentic self after signing your divorce papers. By sharing healthy actions and positive habits from her own experience and her clients' stories, Maureen provides a road map to wholeness for others to "become the archeologist of your own mind" and life. As Maureen says, "You are the best expert in your life. So please, step up and take charge." Read this book. Take charge of your life. By doing so, and following the affirmative practices Maureen so compassionately shares, you will be on your path to a "Hell yes!" kind-of life and will be leaving "Hell no!" to those negative energy drains that hold you back from being all you are meant to be – for you….and your kids!"

– Meaghan E. Mundy, Ph.D.

Coach, Teacher, Whole-Hearted Seeker, meaghanmundy.com

"Each chapter of this book offers personal anecdotes and powerful coaching tools so that the readers can start to change their way of thinking and learn to deal with their ex and co-parent from a place of peace. This book also provides strategies that can be applied to dealing with any challenging situation in life in general; helping readers to set stronger boundaries and find freedom to trust your own emotions and move forward towards a positive resolve. Maureen show readers that ..."Sometimes making one small shift in your mindset can create a ripple effect in your entire life." This book is a beacon of hope for those who find themselves facing the difficult choices in life. Maureen is a bold author who uses her personal experiences to inspire and help others."

– E. Anderson, *Educator*

"This book contains spot-on advice not only for dealing with a difficult ex but for dealing with difficult people in general. As with divorce, many times these people are unavoidable so learning to deal with them on our own terms is liberating and in our best interest. When we practice the strategies that Maureen promotes, the people around us take note particularly our own children who naturally learn these strategies for themselves by watching us. What a wonderful gift for them!"

– D. Reiter, Ph.D.

"12 years post-divorce my ex still doesn't believe that the rules apply to him and surprisingly I was still getting triggered by his rule breaking. Since reading this book, I have begun to make some shifts in the way that I interact with him and most importantly after using the tools that Maureen shared with her readers, I am no longer getting swept up into his crazy, energy draining antics. This book has taught me to remain calm, detach, and to keep my eye on the prize!"

–Sandy Brown

Best Selling Author of Porn Addict's Wife, How to Survive Betrayal and Take Back Your Life

"I don't have children. I had an amicable divorce many years ago and have been married to the love of my life for nearly 21 years. However, I have come to grief from not listening to my body; I have turned control over to people who sucked me dry emotionally. I have been in many situations with people who didn't follow the rules and caused me stress. This book is aimed at women who are having trouble with their ex-husbands, and I am sure that reading this book will help them find peace and clarity. But I would like to recommend Maureen Doyle's strategies to anyone in contact with people who add negativity to their lives."

– S. Frame, *Educator*

"This author's compassion for what you are going through comes through gently in her written voice. It's as though you are there and she is guiding you to make changes that will soften your pain. Her advice is well-tested and it works! It transfers to other situations, as well. I highly recommend this woman's sage advice for this and any other subject she chooses to write about in the future!"

– Amanda von Rosenberg, RDH

"I could not have read this book at a better time! If you can't get along with someone while you're married, there is a good chance matters will only become more difficult after divorce. This book shows that you can't change a manipulative, abusive, narcissistic, argumentative person but you can change your response to those types of people in a way that will ultimately diffuse conflicts & bring you peace. I highly recommend this read if you are struggling to communicate with & rationalize with ANY irrational person...ex-spouse, co-worker, family member, or friend. You will come away with so many lessons & tips to help you set boundaries with toxic people so that their behavior doesn't ultimately damage the quality of your life. Thank you, Maureen, for making this such an easy, relatable read & for sharing your story!"

– G. Nicholl

"I was drawn to this book and I wasn't sure why. I am happily married and the book seemed to be about divorce. What I learned was that this book is about relationships-all relationships. Just reading it helped me find clarity with a friend I'm struggling with. So much good stuff in this little book. Can't recommend it enough."

–Donna Reed, *Mind/Body Coach*

"Reframe your struggles as growth opportunities" these are wise words for dealing with many frustrating situations and people. Maureen Doyle's book is full of strategies to help navigate life with a difficult ex, but they are equally effective for dealing with difficult co-workers, difficult in laws, any difficult people that are hijacking your peace of mind. Her stories, advice and exercises help you to reimagine and rewrite your story, and steer the ship, that is your life, to the island of possibilities – Thank you, Maureen for this powerful little book!"

– T. Ormond, Ph.D.

WHEN YOUR EX DOESN'T FOLLOW THE RULES

WHEN YOUR EX DOESN'T FOLLOW THE RULES

Keep Your Sanity and Raise Happy, Healthy Kids

BY MAUREEN DOYLE

NEW YORK

NASHVILLE • MELBOURNE • VANCOUVER

WHEN YOUR EX DOESN'T FOLLOW THE RULES
Keep Your Sanity and Raise Happy, Healthy Kids

Published in New York, New York, by Morgan James Publishing in partnership with Difference Press. Morgan James is a trademark of Morgan James, LLC. www.MorganJamesPublishing.com

The Morgan James Speakers Group can bring authors to your live event. For more information or to book an event visit The Morgan James Speakers Group at www.TheMorganJamesSpeakersGroup.com.

ISBN 9781683503606 paperback
ISBN 9781683503613 eBook
Library of Congress Control Number: 2016918914

Cover & Interior Design by:
Chris Treccani
www.3dogdesign.net

Editing:
Cynthia Kane

Author's photo courtesy:
K. Doyle Photography

In an effort to support local communities, raise awareness and funds, Morgan James Publishing donates a percentage of all book sales for the life of each book to Habitat for Humanity Peninsula and Greater Williamsburg.

Get involved today! Visit
www.MorganJamesBuilds.com

DEDICATION

For Erin and Máire, of course

TABLE OF CONTENTS

INTRODUCTION

"We must let go of the life that we have planned, so as to accept the one that is waiting for us."
- Joseph Campbell

Marriage was not even on my mind when I met my ex-husband but there was something about him that made me stop in my tracks. He intrigued me. He was a young professional full of intellect and great wit. Dating him was an adventure and I love adventures. Looking back, I probably should have paid closer attention to what might become problems in our future instead of focusing on the fun of the moment.

To the outside world, we had it all but behind closed doors our marriage had become a series of struggles; however, the thought of ending our relationship terrified me since we had children. I had always been able to make decisions easily but this one had me in knots. Literally. My friends told me that my hands used to shake and I had the *"deer in the headlights"* stare. There were many messages along the way that whispered to me to leave but I was committed to the relationship. I began individual counseling and my husband and I also went to couples therapy but not much changed. We were in a bad place and neither of us could see a way out.

Satisfied I had tried everything to save our marriage and convinced we didn't even have a marriage to save, I called my attorney and filed for divorce. I was terrified but I knew it was the right thing to do.

I did not know what was ahead of me but I was certain about what I was leaving behind. I was determined to look forward and not back. I had to be strong for my two girls.

I soon learned that the hardest thing I had to do was not actually get the divorce - it was the years following the divorce. My world was filled with stress, anger, frustration, and costly legal bills. At times I felt like I was drowning and couldn't see a way to save myself, but I knew that I had to not only for me but also for my children. I read countless books, I had meetings with my attorney, I met with counselors, I went to court, I prayed endlessly, and I even dreamed of running away to South America! I asked myself repeatedly during those early years, why couldn't he just follow the rules? Doesn't everyone follow the rules?

Each parent has their own idea and vision of what life will be like post-divorce and chances are that you and your ex will not be in sync on this topic. Many feel that their exes have become more difficult to deal with once the divorce is final: not following the parenting plan, trying to control with financial threats, and expecting flexibility with schedules while not allowing any. I ask my clients all the time, "If your ex-husband was difficult to live with, why on earth would you believe he would be easy to deal with post-divorce?"

Maybe this all sounds familiar to you. Reeling from a high conflict divorce and hopeful now that the court papers are signed and the parenting plan is in place, you can begin to build a life for you and your children. But what you're realizing is that everyone does not follow the rules and it can be a drain on you emotionally, physically, and financially. Visits to your attorney's office occur on a regular basis and on too many occasions, court appearances become the norm. And no one really seems to understand your situation, and certainly not the court system. What can you do? How can you live like this for the next 10 or 15 years? And how can you raise healthy children and begin to create a new life for yourself in the midst of this chaos?

The great news is that you don't have to run off to South America to find the strength to keep going!

As Maya Angelou said, "When you learn, teach." What I've done is taken what I've learned and helped other moms in a similar position.

This book is designed to teach you how to create a wonderful life for you and your family after divorce. I'll walk you through the process so that by the end of the book you will feel empowered, with a clear vision of your future. I have taken my clients through exactly what I'm going to share with you and from this they have gained more confidence in their parenting and in their communication with their exes. They have also learned to trust themselves, stop looking back and start looking forward.

It is my hope that you too will learn how to navigate this crazy journey of co-parenting and how to build a fabulous life for not only you, but also for your children.

I had many sleepless nights but I came to a place of peace with my ex. I know that you can as well. And just remember as the song goes – what doesn't kill you makes you stronger!

CHAPTER 1

Learn To See Clearly

"It's not what you look at that matters,
it is what you see."
- Henry David Thoreau

During the first couple of years after my divorce was final, I remember being completely worn out by my new life. Living in a new place, parenting on my own, following the visitation schedule, and putting out the little fires along the way that surfaced with my children and their father. Every time I felt like I was getting some solid footing on my new life, something would happen that would take away any peace that I was beginning to feel.

Gina's situation was not unique to newly divorced parents. When she came to see me she told me that she was struggling with her ex and co-parenting was a nightmare. Gina asked her ex repeatedly not to share adult topics concerning their relationship and divorce with their children. She pleaded with him that it was not in their best interest. She told him that she had read books about this topic and discussed it with therapists. Gina thought that bringing in experts would appeal to him. Nothing worked. Business as usual. Her ex continued to tell their children anything that he pleased with the hope of hurting her. And little did he care that the ones that he really was hurting were their children. Gina had hoped that conversations with her ex would create change but just wanting something to be different doesn't always translate into results. Gina knew that what she was doing was not working and she was ready to get clear and face her reality and start to make some shifts.

Perhaps you are experiencing a similar frustration now. Many of my clients' stories are sadly the same. Children return home late from visitation, without their belongings, and with their father having told them that the divorce is their mom's fault and that she doesn't want them to have a relationship with dad. And repeated requests to their ex to follow the parenting plan falls on deaf ears.

Sometimes it is the small annoyances that just never seem to cease that can wear you down to seeing the situation for what it really is. And sometimes it is the really big ones that leave you completely drained and wondering if you can go on hoping things will be different for the next 10-15 years.

One of my clients, Sandy, had a very difficult marriage followed by a long and costly divorce. Her ex-husband did not think that the rules applied to him at all. It was not unusual for him to verbally abuse Sandy in front of their young children and he was not concerned who was present. He was a very successful attorney and could be charming when he wanted but he could turn nasty in the very next moment. Sandy was a very trusting and optimistic person so when her ex-husband told her and the courts that he would change his behavior, she believed him. She knew that they would never be friendly with one another but for the sake of their children, she felt that his behavior would improve. She was wrong. This particular evening when he showed up for visitation, he verbally assaulted Sandy and then left with the children.

Sandy lived in a trendy neighborhood that was on the verge of being a very high priced area. You know the neighborhood type – one block has renovated and gorgeous homes and the next street has worn down buildings with tenants that engage in questionable behavior. Sandy had told her children that they were not allowed to walk down that particular street alone. Her ex wanted to cause some chaos that evening after picking up his children and to also undermine Sandy's authority so before he left her home, he told their children that he would wait for them and instructed them to walk around the block – alone. Sandy was outside and heard this conversation. She patiently explained to her ex that it was not a safe area and that she had told them that they could not walk down the street on their own. He ignored her and told the kids to start walking. They were confused and frightened. Why was dad acting so crazy? They began to walk. Being resourceful, Sandy thought that she might as well take a walk around the block and began to follow the kids. That would not work for her ex. He then yelled at the kids to get into the car. They were leaving. They got into the car and he drove off with the car door open and the children had not even had time to buckle their seatbelts. Sandy called the police. It was an easy decision. *It was almost like a light bulb went on and she had clarity about her ex-husband.*

She knew that the car ride to his home would be long and on a highway and she was concerned about them since his behavior was bizarre. While she waited for the police, she walked to the end of the block and saw her ex walking door to door with the children. She approached them and heard that he was asking the neighbors if they thought that it was a safe street for his children. The kids were crying at this point. The police arrived and after a few minutes of conversation, the children were returned to Sandy and visitation was suspended pending a court appearance.

Being in a place of clarity allows you to decide which battles you need to take on and which battles you are just going to have to let go. For Sandy, that night, it was clear. She gave up the fantasy that her ex would put the needs of his children in front of his own desire for control and revenge. Getting clear lets you see the situation for what it is and that makes it easier to deal with. No longer hoping things will change or wishing that they would, you can now meet the situation where it is and respond accordingly. Having this clarity actually helped move Sandy forward and opened up space in her mind so that she could realistically plan and create a new life for herself and her children.

Another client of mine, Emily, felt like from the moment she and her husband walked out of the courtroom, the games began. While she stuck to the parenting plan, her ex behaved like he was unaware that he had even agreed to it. He would call incessantly, be late for visitation regularly, verbally abuse her in front of their children, show up at functions where he was not invited, and basically make her feel on edge the majority of the time. Peace was hard to come by in those early years after the divorce but peace was all that Emily wanted.

During those times, Emily felt like her head was spinning. She was a nervous wreck, always looking over her shoulder and waiting for the next crisis to happen. She began to realize that going to court repeatedly would not get her the peace that she so desperately desired. She knew that she needed to change the way that she was thinking. She had to take a really good look at what she wanted in her life and what she would no longer tolerate. This was her time of awakening. Clarity.

I have many clients come to me at exactly this place in their lives. They have pleaded with their ex-husbands to follow the parenting plan. They have tried to appeal to their ex-husband's sense of right and wrong. They have talked to the lawyers, and they have gone to court. Nothing changes because this behavior is bad but not quite horrible enough for the courts to really do something about it. Here is the thing, what can you do when your ex is not doing something that will wind him up in jail but he is consistently undermining you, making you feel on edge by showing up everywhere, and never paying you on time? How can you create a life of peace for you and your children when you are constantly dealing with this type of behavior? The first step is to get clear on the fact that you can't change his behavior no matter how hard you try. Hoping and wishing for something to be different is not going to change anything.

I had a client, Sarah, who just wanted to be able to take her young son and herself to church each Sunday. She had changed churches since her divorce and longed for the peace that a one hour mass would provide. Her ex-husband spent his Sundays running from one church to the next to try and find her and then position himself in the pew right behind her. Sometimes he would question their child as to what church mom was going to attend that week and other times he would just make the rounds from church to church. Behavior like this just made Sarah on edge and feel unsafe. The message that he was sending was clear, "you might have divorced me but you will never feel safe again."

What did she do? She spent many hours in her attorney's office and letters were drafted and motions were sent to the courthouse. Unless something big occurs, like physical abuse, the courts can tell someone to stop their behavior, but in reality, it is very difficult to get them to stop and to follow the rules. What can you do?

Maybe you are in this place now, trying to appeal to your ex as a decent human being. Are you getting anywhere? Is it exhausting? How about trying something new? Let go of the fantasy of peaceful co-parenting and become clear about your life. Only when you see your life clearly for what it is right now, can you make positive moves toward a better future.

Let's get some clarity around your current situation and look at it with a new set of eyes. Make a list of what your ex-husband was like before/during your marriage and post-divorce. Maybe your list looks something like this.

Before/During Your Marriage
- Controlling
- Manipulative
- Self-serving
- Dismissive
- Prone to temper tantrums
- Dishonest
- Can be quite charming

Post-Divorce
- Controlling
- Manipulative
- Self-serving
- Dismissive
- Prone to temper tantrums
- Dishonest
- Can be quite charming

Now your turn –

Before/During Your Marriage

- _____
- _____
- _____
- _____

- _____
- _____
- _____

Post-Divorce

- _____
- _____
- _____
- _____
- _____
- _____
- _____

What does your list look like? Has he changed? Are you going to hold your breath hoping that he will change? This is your reality and the reality that your children are dealing with each day. What are you going to do with this information? Stop trying to change him. Stop trying to make him be a good parent. Stop holding onto hope. Face your reality.

> _"The first step toward change is awareness._
> _The second step is acceptance."_
> **- Nathaniel Branden**

Let's look at what you need to change in order to bring some peace into your life. What do you have control over? What do you want? When I discuss this with my clients, we always start out with making a list of what they do not want in their lives.

Then we move over to what they do want in their lives. Finally we explore what changes they can make right now.

Get Clear to Get Clarity Exercise

What I *do not* want –

- Late visitation pickups and drop offs
- Late monthly support payments
- Ex bad mouthing me to our children

- _____
- _____
- _____
- _____

What I *do* want –

- On time visitation pickups and drop offs
- On time monthly support payments
- No more bad mouthing of me by ex

- _____
- _____
- _____
- _____

Now look at your list and ask yourself –

How can I make a positive change to get what I need without a battle?

What I *can* change -

- Make changes to the visitation plan to limit contact with my ex and remove opportunities for him to disrupt my schedule
- Go to family court and ask that the monthly support payments be sent directly to me through a garnishment of my ex-husband's wage and remove my ex from the process
- Let my children know that it is always unacceptable to be mean and call others names.
- _____
- _____
- _____
- _____

I always encourage my clients to tell their children "I don't know why Daddy would say that about me. I am sorry that you had to hear that." And then drop it. (You might want to document it for your records)

For one of my clients, she wanted some peace around visitation drop offs. Her ex was notorious for bringing the children back to her late on Sunday nights without any of their schoolwork completed. She decided to make a change to the parenting plan and have her children stay with their dad on Sunday nights and have him bring the children to school on Monday morning. She hated to lose time with her children on Sunday nights but she realized that Sunday evenings actually were quite stressful with the way that they had been going and she made a very good decision not only for herself but also for her children. She made the choice to stop the madness around Sunday nights and create peace. Her ex-husband might have believed that he had won some victory over having the children on an extra evening but she knew the truth that peace had been created. She kept her *eye on the prize* and for her that was having a peaceful life for her and her children. She chose not to engage in any more battles around Sunday evenings.

The months and years following a divorce can make you feel like you are on a roller coaster ride. There are so many twists and turns and ups and downs and it can leave you feeling disoriented and exhausted. And this is with an ex that follows the rules. What if your ex does not? There is hope but the first step is getting clear. Get off of the amusement park ride for a moment, take a deep breath, and look at your situation.

Become the Compassionate Observer of Your Life

- Place yourself high on a hill and look down on a scene from your life. What do you see? Describe it.
- _____
  _____
  _____
  _____
  _____
  _____
  _____
  _____

_____

_____

- Who is there? What is happening?

_____

_____

_____

_____

_____

_____

_____

_____

_____

- Go to a place of being curious about this scene without judgment and without emotion. *Become the compassionate observer.*
- What would you tell that single mother to do?

_____

_____

_____

_____

_____

_____

_____

_____

_____

_____

_____

- Where can she make some changes in her life?

_____
_____
_____
_____
_____
_____
_____
_____
_____

When we become the compassionate observer, we remove ourselves from our daily situation and are able to look at it with a fresh set of eyes. We are able to view our lives with more clarity and we are able to craft some creative solutions to our problems. Use this exercise when you are particularly stuck in a situation and it is hard for you to see your way out. You will be surprised with what your compassionate observer has to say to you!

Begin to make small changes toward peace and calmness in your home. Make it a refuge for you and your children. Fill your home with routine, laughter, love, safety and happiness. When you get clear on what you want and what you will no longer tolerate, you will begin to feel more confidence and strength. Your children are watching you - you are the model of appropriate behavior with difficult people. Some days may be easier than others but keep moving forward. When you put your head down on the pillow at night, you can tell yourself that you did the right thing, you have your honor and integrity and that you kept your eye on the prize.

CHAPTER 2

Begin To Trust Yourself

"Our inner guidance comes to us through our feelings and body wisdom first – not through intellectual understanding."

- Christiane Northrup

We live in a very noisy world with many voices competing to be heard. There is society, friends, coworkers, family and then of course the voices in your head. When you are single parenting, add to that your ex, the lawyers and the courts. It can be a very confusing place to be. Decisions become hard to make and leave you feeling dizzy, unclear, and anxious. What can you do? Where can you turn?

How about bringing in that beautiful ally and trusted friend called your body. Your intuition, that little voice inside of you. Your spiritual guide that is always there for you, waiting to be consulted, longing to be heard and its only purpose is to guide you toward what is best for you. Do you recognize this tiny voice? Do you notice that you are being guided? Do you listen?

I was a teacher for many years and observed that young children rely much more on their intuition than adults. They follow what feels good and move away from what doesn't feel good. And young children certainly don't judge or second-guess themselves. Sounds really logical and easy. Too bad that many of us forget that as we get older. We begin to invite others into our decision-making and we also bring in our intellect and slowly start to turn a deaf ear to the wisdom of our bodies, our intuition and our spiritual guides.

When I introduced this idea to a client, Cindy, she told me immediately, "I am not an intuitive person and I have no idea how to tap into this nor do I really trust that it would even work for me." Cindy is not alone. In our modern society, we have been taught to rely on our intellect and ignore other methods for seeking guidance and answers. As a single parent, the amount of decisions that you have to make on your own and very often in an adversarial environment is enormous. It is imperative to have all of your sources of support and enlightenment at your side, fully engaged, and at your disposal. But how do you get there? All it takes is an open mind and some practice.

One way that our intuition sends us messages is through physical sensations. Our shoulders become tense and ache, we get headaches, and we feel exhausted. Or we feel light, airy, and energized.

Sometimes my clients get confused with nervous feelings – butterflies in their stomach. They wonder if their intuition is trying to tell them something.

"Should I be changing directions? Are my nervous feelings showing up because I am not doing what is best for me or is it just normal nervous feelings associated with doing something different and unfamiliar?"

We all get those sensations in our stomachs when we try something new but the important thing is to distinguish between the feelings of *Hell Yes* with the feelings of *Hell No!*

As bestselling author and life coach Martha Beck puts it, when we ask our body to help us with a decision, does it feel like "Shackles on or shackles off?" When we are following what is best for us, it always feels like shackles off. It feels like freedom and you might feel light and expansive. Shackles on feels like prison and poison.

Charlotte came to me struggling with the many decisions that she had to make as a single parent. We talked about tapping into the wisdom of her body for guidance. This was a new concept for Charlotte so we went back in time to discover that her body had been trying to communicate with her for a very long time. We talked about when she first met her husband and how she felt in her body. She told me that he fascinated her. He had great intellect, high energy, and was very ambitious. She did what she had always done in the past and that was to follow what intrigued her. And he really intrigued her! What she did not do was listen to her intuition. She did not listen to her body, which was screaming at her to run the other way. Thinking back, she remembers feeling tense around him or having stomachaches when they were together. Charlotte dismissed those physical sensations. Charlotte felt on some level that they were *not a match made in heaven* but she was determined to continue with the relationship because she could intellectualize why he was the perfect catch.

When we don't listen to the whispers that our bodies are sending to us, it has to amp it up to try and get our attention!

So the whispers became louder for Charlotte. She experienced severe back pain for the first time in her life. She couldn't walk for a week but again she chose to ignore it and believed that it was nothing more than her back giving her a hard time. Her ex-husband looked great on paper and her mind was telling her that being with him was a great decision. She neglected to listen to her body, her intuition, and the messages that were coming to her through physical pain.

When in your life has your body been trying to get your attention and send you messages that you need to make some changes? How was it trying to speak to you? Did you experience any of these symptoms?

- Back pain
- Tense, achy shoulders
- Intestinal Problems
- Heart Palpitations
- Headaches

- Panic Attacks
- Extreme fatigue

Think about your life at that time. What was going on?

_____

_____

_____

_____

_____

_____

_____

_____

Was your intuition trying to get your attention? Did you listen? What was the outcome?

_____

_____

_____

_____

_____

_____

_____

_____

Sometimes we ignore the whispers that our bodies are telling us because we want to please others and avoid being judged by our friends and loved ones. Sometimes it is the judgment of society that we fear the most. We'd rather disappoint ourselves than the people around us. That can only work for so long because living a life that is a lie will eventually catch up with us and those whispers that are trying to get our attention will eventually turn into shouts.

Where in your life are you living out of alignment?
- Doing what you *should do* and not what you *want to do?*
- Allowing your ex to run the show?
- Not speaking up about what is best for you? For your children?
- Keeping your opinions and your desires to yourself so as to not rock the boat?

And here is the big one –
- Are you afraid of being labeled as the *bitch* even though you know that you are just telling your truth - just saying what is best for you and what is best for your children?

As you navigate this journey of single parenting, your decisions are not going to please everyone. There will be critics. There will be people who offer unsolicited advice. Get used to it. Some are doing it because they genuinely care about you. Others are doing it simply because they feel like they are the expert of your life. Whatever the reason that is their business and the best policy is to listen to what they have to say. Ponder it. Examine it. Take the good and leave behind the bad and don't look back or second-guess yourself.

When I was in this place many years ago, a very wise psychologist told me "Ignore what those people are saying to you about what you should be doing. How do they know what you are experiencing? How do they know what is best for you? How could they possibly? No one knows, no one can really know. Only you know and you are the best expert on what is right for you." I always carried those words with me and pulled them out every time someone would offer their opinions or advice. I would smile, listen, and then go do what I knew was the right thing to do for my children and me. I knew that I was the only one that really knew the right decision.

Now don't get me wrong. I am a firm believer that *knowledge is power*. And I do my research. I am a major fact finder. But then there is the time to stop doing the research, stop looking outside for answers and turn inward. You are the best expert of your life so please step up and take charge. If you don't there is always someone who will take that role for you.

One of my clients, Michele, was married to a very controlling husband, Steve. Decisions were always made by him and Michele learned to not question him. She thought that it was best to just go along rather than create waves. Throughout her marriage, Michele suffered from migraines. When Steve fell in love with a coworker and filed for divorce, Michele was lost. She had given away all of her power to this man for so many years and now she was on her own with three young children. She needed to start making decisions for herself and her kids. The thought of it was overwhelming and because of habit and her comfort level, more often than not, she would let her ex-husband call all of the shots. But something started to stir in Michele. She grew weary of this arrangement and noticed that her body felt uneasy and heavy when her ex made all of the decisions. Michele wanted to jump into the arena and make her own decisions, but she was anxious to assert her authority. She started slowly. She began to find her voice and began to speak louder. I told Michele that her voice had not been used for so long that it was like a muscle that had not been worked. It was weak but by exercising it daily, it would become stronger. Michele started to tell her ex-husband her opinions on their children and her frustrations when he did not follow the parenting plan. At first, Steve was not happy with the new Michele and would fight her to maintain his position as the decision maker but slowly he began to realize that this new version of Michele was not going away. He began to realize that she was no longer a woman that he could just boss around; she was a woman to respect. As Michele's voice grew stronger and stronger, her migraines went away.

Another client, Kathy, came to me because she was unhappy in her marriage and she was struggling with her health. We talked about her life and her marriage and she described all of it from an intellectual point of view. She was married to a successful doctor and he gave her and their children everything that they could ever want, except he could be very demeaning and verbally abusive to Kathy. She gave excuses for her husband treating her badly. "He was stressed out and he had a hard childhood," she told me. I asked her how she felt when she was with him. She told me that her stomach was in knots. She said that when he opened the garage door at night, she could feel her body become tense. She would feel sick to her stomach. She knew that this was a horrible way to live, but she was committed to her marriage and her family. Even though her current situation was difficult, the thought of making any changes to it were terrifying.

I asked Kathy to tell me more about the messages that her body had been sending her over the years. She had intestinal problems and had back surgery several years earlier. I asked her to describe moments in her life when she felt light and free in her body. Kathy told me that she felt great on her last vacation with her daughter, alone. She told me that she felt wonderful and was free of stomach pains when she visited a favorite coastal city by herself. Kathy began to realize that her body had incredible wisdom and that she had been ignoring this for years. The mind can play tricks on us but the body will never lie. Kathy began to appreciate her body for being her truth meter and really started to listen to it. She also began to make some big changes in her life. Kathy began speaking up for herself with her husband and insisted that they go to couples therapy. She told him that the way that he had been treating her was completely unacceptable and that she would no longer tolerate it. Her husband responded positively to the new Kathy and their relationship improved. The fear that had kept Kathy in her abusive relationship was now replaced with a new sense of confidence. When Kathy now needs to make a decision that involves her husband, she thinks about her options but then she checks in with her body as well. Following her intuition and coupling it with her intellect proves to be a great method of dealing with all decisions in her life. It is like having a trusted friend for advice when she needs it.

God has given us both great intellect and intuition. But do you use both? I know that I did not. It was much easier to do that when I was younger and only in my mid 20's did I start to ignore the wisdom of my body and begin to rely solely on my mind. And I know that I am not alone. How many individuals have had heart attacks or develop serious illnesses after years of living in an unhealthy relationship, working at a job that sucks the life from them, or continuing to battle with an ex-husband that has no regard for the parenting plan or the law?

You may have forgotten to use your body as a compass for moving toward what is right for you and walking away from danger but it is never too late to start to tap into its wisdom again. One of the benefits of rediscovering this for yourself is that you will be modeling this for your children. Wouldn't it be wonderful for your kids to learn to trust their intuition, their inner guidance? As my own daughters reached the age of going off to college, I insisted that they read, *The Gift of Fear,* by Gavin de Becker. In this book, de Becker tells readers to trust their gut instincts and act on them. He gives great examples of how people have either walked into precarious situations when their gut told them to run the other way or how people have listened to that inner voice and moved away from risky situations. I gave it to my children with the hope that they would continue to trust that voice inside to avoid danger when they went off into the world.

Now that you are aware that your body is sending you signals, how can you incorporate this into your daily living? Awareness is certainly the first step.

- Start to listen to your body. Really listen to it.
- Each morning, take a few minutes to scan your body starting at your toes and move through your body.
- What do you feel? Some aches and pains are familiar and could just represent old injuries.

- Notice the more subtle feelings.
  - » Do you feel tense in your stomach?
  - » Do you have a headache?
- Close your eyes and ask yourself what your body is trying to tell you. Take deep breaths. Wait for the messages. Ask for guidance. Trust and the answers will come.

The body can be a great companion in life to help direct us where we need to go but there are other guides. Our intuition will speak to us through blogs that appear in our email, through books that jump off the shelves as we walk through stores, through sermons that seem like they were written and delivered just for us or through conversations with strangers that point us in a new direction. We also receive messages from the divine through thoughts that just pop into our minds.

Be open to the possibilities that are endless when you believe that the universe, your spiritual connection, your intuition, is trying to connect with you and help guide you. When you get to this place of noticing and expecting messages to come, that is when the world seems magical. But how can we get to this place when all we hear is noise around us?

> "If you consciously let your body take care of you, it will become your greatest ally and trusted partner."
> – **Deepak Chopra**

Several years ago, I was preparing to go to court with my ex-husband and I was a nervous wreck. I went to my place of peace to try to calm down. I went to mass.

I became really quiet and dropped into a place of wordlessness.

- I asked for guidance.
- I asked for support.
- I waited.

The church started to sing –

> *"Be not afraid, I go before you always. Come follow me, and I will give you rest"*

A rush of peace came over me and I knew that I could handle my court appearance on that day and that all would be well. I felt guided that day. I felt completely supported from a place outside of my physical world.

Dropping into a place of wordlessness. What does that mean? It is a place where I attempt to quiet my mind and observe my body and wait for answers. Did I somehow intuitively know how to do this? Not at all. I felt like I was not really a person that could meditate; I have so much energy and sitting in a place and just focusing on my breathing seemed like prison. All that I wanted to do was to keep moving. Lots of nervous energy. So I developed my own way to drop into wordlessness so I could tap into God, the universe, my body and get some answers to help me with my chaotic life. This was the method that I developed while attending daily mass.

I would take a deep breath in and say –

> *"Breathe in the Holy Spirit"* and then exhale,
> *"Breathe out my humanity"*.

This mediation worked for me because I knew I needed extra help with my journey and the extra help would need to come from the spiritual realm.

So there you go. This was my way to calm myself, get out of my head, and unite with the spirit and body. I found that this short phrase coupled with slowing my breathing really quieted my mind and relaxed me. Find what works for you. Find a place to practice dropping into wordlessness and find that connection. Find a phrase that can move you into that space. And then practice it.

Once I mastered this, I was able to do this without anyone even knowing that I was going there. It came in handy when I found myself in court or facing a difficult situation with my ex.

I have a client, Donna, who has been trying to co-parent with an ex-husband who is a raging narcissist. Every day there seems to be another struggle and he seems to engage her in these conflicts just for sport! Just to make her life difficult. He draws her into his crazy world and quite often she finds herself confused about what she should do. We have worked on trusting her body for answers and this has become her method for dealing with her ex and making decisions. She begins with quieting her mind and slowing down her breathing. Next she imagines the entire scenario that she is considering. She stays there for a few minutes and checks in with her body to see how it feels. Does her body feel light and airy? Or does it feel heavy and miserable. She then asks herself, "What would be best for my daughter?"

I remind her to remove her ex from the equation to keep her focus on what would be best for her daughter. When Donna couples her intellect with the wisdom of her body, she always feels like she has made the right decision. She has told me that following this system has made decision making with her ex less stressful. Before her mind would race and it was difficult for her to find clarity but now she has found greater peace in decision-making.

Perhaps you find yourself in a struggle to make a decision. You think about it from all different angles and you cannot come to a resolution. You look for outside answers, you look to Google, and you find yourself getting more confused. Why not pair up your mind and your body to find the answer? Trusting yourself begins with asking yourself what is best for you, getting really quiet, listening for the answers, and then moving forward. It is about getting out of your head and checking in with your body, your intuition, and then moving toward your best life. We need to trust that we are the best experts for what we need to do in our lives and remember to use one of our greatest gifts for guidance, our intuition. Stop looking for outside approval and validation and start looking inward. Once you do you'll be able to make the best decisions for you and your children after divorce.

CHAPTER 3

Melt Your Mind Chatter

"The mind is everything,
What you think you become."
- Buddha

t has been said that we have anywhere between 50,000 –
70,000 thoughts a day. That is around 35 thoughts per
minute. When I heard that statistic, I had a difficult time
believing it but when I paid attention I was suddenly aware of
the many thoughts rushing through my mind. "Oh, I love that
outfit that she is wearing, I wonder if it would look good on me,
where did she get it? Man, the sun is so bright today, I wish I
had my sunglasses, I'm feeling hungry, should I go home to eat

or just stop here for a quick bite? I really need to phone back my mom, but I hope she doesn't keep me on the phone. My ex is driving me crazy. Can he just do what he is supposed to do today?" Wow! You get the picture. The thoughts never cease. Our minds are just an-out-of-control thought generator. And that is fine just as long as those thoughts are supporting and encouraging us and not just bringing us down.

Many of our thoughts are merely observations about our daily life and are harmless. But then there are the thoughts that can be detrimental to our soul. It has been said that ninety-five percent of our thoughts are repeated daily and become our mindset. Is your mindset limiting your potential, holding you back, or beating you up? The sad truth is that many of those 50,000 daily thoughts are actually focused on the past or the future and can fall into the categories of making you feel guilty about some past action, worry about your future, or beat yourself up for some real or perceived shortcoming. When it comes to your divorce and to your ex, are your thoughts helping or hurting you? Are you constantly worrying about your future, which keeps you from enjoying the present? Or becoming preoccupied with what your ex has done or might do which keeps you in a state of perpetual fear and anxiety? How do these thoughts affect your daily life? How do they affect your relationship with your children?

Don't you think that it is time to take control? Imagine what it would feel like if you could stop the voices in your head that tell you that your life is over because of the divorce, that you will never get back on track, and that your ex will always create havoc in your life. What would that look like for you? For me it meant that I could fill my mind with positive images of my future and create space for dreams and possibilities but only if I could let go of the thoughts of fear and worry.

The first step is awareness. What am I telling myself? What is going on in my mind? By the end of this chapter, you'll recognize the thoughts that are holding you back from living the life you want after your divorce and you'll know how to change them.

I never really knew the power of my thoughts – both good and bad. Sure, I knew that sometimes I could be very positive with myself but there were other times when I could treat myself pretty crappy. I never really questioned them and just accepted that they were just a part of life. I let them all coexist. It was only when I started my coach training that I really began to examine my thoughts and discovered that many of them were just mean and were not serving me. I also learned that thoughts are only true if I believed them.

At the time, I was a schoolteacher. Teachers have a difficult job of having to answer to many different customers. They have to answer to the administration, the parents, and the students. I was a new teacher and had many limiting thoughts running through my mind. "I am not an expert in science, how in the world can I teach the material? Everyone knows that you are an imposter, you can't really teach anything. No one will listen to you. The parents are all scientists from a local research hospital and they know way more than you! Get out now before everyone discovers that you are not qualified!" Oh, the list of thoughts went on and on.

When it came to single parenting, I had a similar list of thoughts

- I made the wrong decision to get a divorce, this is way too hard
- People will judge me because I am a single parent
- I can't do this alone
- I will end up with nothing and have to live on the street
- I am too old to start over again
- I am too stupid to get a new career going

Back then, my mind was not a fun place to be! And I could get very creative in dreaming up beliefs that kept me in a place of helplessness and despair. How about these?

- What if the divorce will destroy my children?
- What if my daughters become high school dropouts?
- What if I can never find love again?
- What if it is too late for me to follow my dreams?
- What if my ex remarries and his wife is a monster to my children?

The *What if's* can really get your head spinning!

One of my clients, Rachel, had a list of thoughts that she carried around that were really holding her back and leaving her in a place of constant panic. When we met, we began to excavate some of these nasty critters. Here are some of the top ten hits that kept playing in her head.

- I can't handle being a single mom
- My ex is going to destroy me (financially, emotionally)
- I am 40 years old and no one will ever want to date me
- I am so fat and I will always be alone
- I am not smart enough to go back into the work force

The tunes played on and on in her head. As we began to pull all of these out of her mind, Rachel was amazed at how many of her thoughts were negative and really unkind. She was aware that she walked around with some negative thoughts but the volume and severity of them shocked her. We then tried to look around for the positive thoughts. They were harder to find and fewer in number. She also felt uncomfortable verbalizing those to me. Isn't it amazing that we are so much more at ease talking about ourselves negatively than positively?

> *"Change your thoughts*
> *and you change your world."*
> **- Norman Vincent Peale**

Perhaps you too are walking around with a whole playlist of negative thoughts. Are those messages advancing you forward toward a life of joy and ease? Or are they holding you back in a place where you can't seem to move under the weight of them? So what can you do? It all begins with awareness. Stop for a moment and notice the sheer volume of the thoughts floating around in your mind. Next start to grab these thoughts and examine them. Bring them out of the darkness and into the light. Don't let them hide out in your mind and secretly sabotage you.

We can never change what we do not acknowledge so becoming really clear and honest about the negativity that inhabits our mind is the first step to releasing the hold that they have on our lives.

Take a moment in your day to do a thought download. Get yourself a dedicated notebook or journal and start with the date on the top of the page. And then just let all of the thoughts flow from your mind to pen to paper. No judgment, no editing. Let it rip. I like to do this in the morning before my day gets hectic. You can accomplish this in only a few minutes.

When I began to do this, I was amazed at the number of negative thoughts that had taken up residence in my mind. I am sure that you will be surprised as well. But for right now, you are just an investigator. See what appears. Try to make this a daily practice for the next month. I promise that you will be surprised by your findings. I am sure that some thoughts will be quite familiar because you have carried them around for years. Others might be new and shocking. Take on the role of the scientist and gather your data.

Each day, after you have your thoughts down on paper, take a few minutes to challenge them. Ask yourself if they are true. Ask yourself if they are helping in your journey or are they holding you back. Thoughts are not true unless you believe them. Just because you think them does not make them real. And this is the really interesting part: the brain will always find evidence to support your thoughts whether they are good or bad. So decide for yourself, what thoughts are you going to support?

Let's take a look back at Rachel's negative thoughts
- I can't handle being a single mom

- My ex is going to destroy me (financially, emotionally)
- I am 40 years old and no one will ever want to date me
- I am so fat and I will always be alone
- I am not smart enough to go back into the work force

I asked Rachel if she believed that her thoughts were true. She did. Then I asked her if they are helpful. She knew that they were not helpful. Now we were getting somewhere. Finally, I told Rachel to *Flip the Thought*. Make the statement opposite.

Let's look at Rachel's thoughts again but as the opposite.
- *I can handle being a single mom*
- *My ex is not going to destroy me (financially, emotionally)*
- *I am 40 years old and someone, in fact many men, will want to date me*
- *I am not fat and I will not be alone*
- *I am smart enough to go back into the work force*

Rachel read these new thoughts and began to smile. She really had not realized how her thoughts were bringing her down on a daily basis. After she did this exercise for one month, she began to see some changes in her life. She slowly began to lose weight and started to date. The important thing is that she was no longer being terrorized by her own thoughts. Every day we have a choice. Do you want to be your own cheerleader or your own bully? What do you choose?

Thoughts are powerful. They can bring us up or they can tear us down. Sometimes it is difficult to acknowledge that you have thoughts living in your mind that are not supporting you. What is another way that you can find out if this is happening? How can you know if you are walking around with an overabundance of crappy thoughts? Look to your feelings. How do you feel?

Positive, happy, energetic, optimistic, creative, resourceful
or
Negative, sad, depleted, pessimistic, stuck

Your feelings can be a great indicator that you could be carrying around some nasty thoughts.

Susan came to me shortly after her divorce. She was enthusiastic about her new life and was anxious to get it started but she felt like every time she moved two steps forward, she took three steps back. Her ex-husband was always causing some form of trouble in her and her son's life. She felt sad, defeated, and exhausted and could not see a light at the end of the tunnel. Susan and I talked about how her feelings were an indication that she probably was carrying around some negative thoughts. At one of our sessions, Susan began to talk and I began to take notes. When she had finished I showed her the list of thoughts that were flying out of her mouth.

- I will never be free of this chaos
- Everyone thinks that I am crazy
- I am a failure
- I have no control
- My son has no respect for me
- There is not enough time

Susan's list was even longer than you see here. It was surprising to her. Some of her thoughts were familiar to her. She had been hearing them for years and others were new since her divorce. Susan wanted more energy and positivity in her life and was ready to try new things. We started with her negative thoughts. I explained to her that repetitive thoughts make ruts in our brains called neuropathways and since our brains are very efficient, these old thoughts will continue to run over and over again unless she did something about it. She needed to challenge the thoughts that bring her pain and then replace them with new thoughts that would make her feel better. Susan began to notice her thoughts on her daily download and began to flip them. Slowly the old thoughts began to lose power and the new thoughts started to gain strength. After doing this for a few months, Susan found more energy and was able to approach her single parenting with greater confidence and ease.

The mind can be a very dangerous place. It is a thought factory that has no limits.

We all carry around numerous negative beliefs that hold us back and sabotage our happiness. And add to that our creativity that can dream up some pretty elaborate scenarios where we have no control and are trapped in a prison of our own making.

The truth is that we always have a choice. We can always choose whether or not to believe our thoughts. My hope for you is that you become the archeologist of your own mind and start to dig around and discover the thoughts that are limiting you. Get them out on the table and examine them. Let go of the ones that are holding you back or keeping you in a rut. Replace them with thoughts that support your dreams. Your new life as a single parent depends on you busting up these thought patterns. This is the perfect time for you to take inventory of your life. What do you want to keep around? What can you throw away? Begin with the crappy thoughts that do not serve you and never have.

CHAPTER 4

Anger, Friend or Foe?

*"Bitterness is like cancer. It eats upon the host.
But anger is like fire. It burns it all clean."*
- Maya Angelou

A nger gets such a bad rap. Some people try to avoid it at all costs while others point fingers and criticize those who show this essential emotion. But anger is actually neutral. It isn't good; it isn't bad. It is what you do with it that matters. You can use it to build or to destroy. It is your choice.

Anger can be a helpful tool to use to get us moving or to solve a problem. I use my anger as an indication that something in my life needs my attention. It is a motivating force and it gives me a tremendous amount of positive energy. When I feel the bubbling up of fury inside of me, I know that I am about to take action.

One of my clients, Eileen, used her anger as a call to action. He ex-husband paid her child support late every month. Whether it was three days or three weeks late, it was a monthly occurrence. Not only that, she had to remind her ex each month to pay his obligation. This went on for a year. Initially Eileen played along with this game. She had grown weary of going to court and wanted to avoid conflict. But slowly her frustration grew. Her anger grew. And her anger finally motivated Eileen to make a change. She called her attorney and went to court. The judge admonished her ex and told him to start paying on time and that the next time that he was late on his court ordered support payment, he would be put into jail. He was never late again.

Can you think of a situation with your ex-husband that causes your blood pressure to rise and your teeth to clench? Instead of ignoring it or letting it smolder, can you do something about it? Is it your call to action? Are you so tired of dealing with something that you are ready to do something about it? Maybe it is time to take that step. Let anger be your fuel to get you moving toward a resolution.

There is another type of anger but it is toxic. It is the type that wears you down and leaves you lying on the coach with a splitting headache. Sometimes you don't know what just hit you and other times all you can do is think about hitting someone or something!

Early on in single parenting, there seemed to be one battle after another with my ex-husband and I felt like my body was constantly being drained. I knew that I did not want to live like this but I really was not sure how to change it. I just desperately needed to make a shift. This perpetual state of frustration and anger was robbing me of my joy and my focus. I began to notice people that raged on and on. Their anger was deadly and surely it was affecting their health. These people didn't use anger as a tool to help them move forward but rather it seemed to keep them stuck in a place of constant conflict. They seemed to be controlled by anger instead of being in control. I did not want any of that. A wise counselor helped me move from a place of constantly being drawn into battle with my ex by using a rope as a visual tool. I have since used this with my clients and it has been so successful. Notice how it helped my client, Lisa.

Lisa came to me soon after her divorce and she was completely overwhelmed and exhausted by her ex-husband, Joe. Co-parenting with him was anything but peaceful. Joe knew how to rile up Lisa and he seemed to take pleasure in it. When he came to pick up their children, he would make insulting remarks to Lisa, but not in front of others or the children. He was very stealth with his insults. His words were always meant to tear her down and he was an expert on making her feel bad about herself. He commented on her physically, he commented on her parenting skills, and he commented on her family. "Looks like you are gaining some weight! Watch out for that! You really are a horrible parent and everyone knows that! Your family is pathetic. No one in your family has ever been truly successful!" The insults went on and on. Sometimes, Lisa could ignore these horrible remarks, and other times, she just wanted to strangle him! Sometimes she could keep her mouth shut and other times, she blasted him. How could she keep quiet? He was not only insulting her but he was also insulting her family. The truth was that Lisa's ex was baiting her and was hoping to get her upset. And at times, she obliged. And that thrilled him. He won. He would leave with the children with a smile on his face and Lisa was left depleted.

I gave Lisa a rope. I held onto one end and gave her the other end. I asked her to pull on the rope really hard. I did the same. I pulled her toward me. There was a lot of tension on that rope. I explained to Lisa that this is what happens every time her ex pulls her into an argument. He dangles the rope in front of her and she grabs onto it. She willingly participates in his game.

Next I told her to let go of the rope. No more tension. No more being dragged along by her ex. When she dropped the rope, he lost his power. No more game. No more fun for him.

She became angry when she thought about how many times he baited her and how she allowed it to happen. Lisa used her anger to motivate her to make some changes around visitation pickups and drop offs. She decided to limit her exposure to her ex during these pickups and when he dropped the rope in front of her the next time, she would refuse to grab it. She made a commitment to herself that afternoon to no longer be a willing participant in his tug-of-war game.

Can you think of a time when your ex has dangled the rope in front of you? Did you grab it? Did you let him drag you along? It is pretty easy to engage in this energy sucking game particularly because you might be defending yourself, your parenting, your children, and your family. But what are you really gaining? When you grab the rope, he is in charge. He has the power. Take back your power. Don't grab the rope. Now you are in charge.

Anger is not the only robber of our energy. Another energy drain can be less obvious but over time, it can be just as lethal. Sometimes the *Energy Vampires* in our lives can suck the life force out of us with their fear, anger, criticism, narcissism, or neediness. Look around – we all have them. They can be friends, family, co-workers, or our ex-husbands. These individuals will gladly take all of your positive energy and feed on it leaving you feeling empty.

Perhaps your ex is an energy vampire and thrives on being negative and difficult. He loves to draw you into his dramatic stories. Many times, his tales don't involve you and you feel relieved that he has turned his attention and criticism elsewhere but you still feel exhausted after being with him. Your head is spinning. How can you protect yourself from this energy theft?

Stacy had been divorced for three years and had gotten to a place of relative peace with her ex. The process was difficult and she had her share of big battles but life had begun to feel pretty good. There was a problem however that still lingered. Every time that Stacy was in the presence of her ex she felt a low level of irritation and incredible fatigue. Why did she feel this way? He wasn't attacking her nor was he being rude to her. The conversations seemed innocent enough but as Stacy thought about it, she realized that they always seemed to focus on conflicts with others, lack of money, or some impending doom. Absent were the uplifting stories. Nothing positive was ever mentioned. After an encounter with him, Stacy felt depleted.

How did he do that? And more importantly, how could she protect herself from her ex stealing her precious energy?

The thing is, relationships, are always an exchange of energy. People can either lift you up or they drain you. In Stacy's case, her relationship with her ex was only one sided. He had the power to siphon all of her positive energy in a 15-minute period! When Stacy looked around, she noticed that she had other energy vampires in her life as well. I told her what worked for me.

I thought about Pope John Paul riding around in his Popemobile. He had a glass shield that surrounded him for protection. Everyone could see him but he was safeguarded from harm within his Popemoblile. Whenever I met with the energy vampires in my life, I imagined being surrounded by my very own Popemobile. I was able to participate in a conversation but my energy was shielded behind the glass. Nothing and no one could take it away from me. I became very good at carrying around my shield like a bubble of protection.

Stacy imagined that she was surrounded by a bright light that protected her from the energy thieves in her life. When she encountered her ex-husband and he would begin to tell tales of how awful the world was, she would politely smile, take some deep breaths, and turn on her energetic shield of bright light. Her energy was being safely protected.

Next time you find yourself with your ex-husband who wants to rope you into an argument or an energy vampire that wants to suck the life from you, try these strategies. They worked for my clients and me.

- Limit your time with them. Tell them up front what time you need to leave and stick to it.
- Keep your sentences short and remain on topic.
- Maintain a business like tone when communicating with them.
- When insults come your way, try this response "I am sorry that you feel that way" and don't engage.
- Use creative visualizations. One of my client's favorite was imagining her ex's face on a TV screen. His mouth was going a mile a minute but she had switched on the MUTE button. She saw his lips moving but she was not listening to his words at all. She tuned in when she needed to but ignored the rest.
- And don't forget to bring along your protective shield!

As a single parent, remember that your energy is a precious commodity and it is something that you should conserve so please do not give it up to your ex or to the energy vampires in your life. Release it only when necessary - use your very helpful emotion, anger, sparingly. Don't get caught up in the game of trying to get back at your ex-husband. When you do that, he is taking your attention and sucking up your energy. You are divorced from him and it is time for you to focus your energy on yourself and your children. Place your attention on creating something wonderful instead of trying to bring him down. Does he deserve your consideration? Does he deserve your time? Your energy? Hasn't he already taken enough of it?

CHAPTER 5

Know What You Can Control

"You can't control other people,
You can only control your reactions to them."
- Unknown

ife after divorce is filled with uncertainty and change. There are so many decisions to make. Where should I live? When should I get a job? Where should I work? Should I go back to school for more education? And those are the easy ones. They involve only you. Then there are other daily thoughts that seem to fill our minds and ultimately keep us stuck and unable to begin a new life.

- How can I start my life when my ex keeps me going back to court?
- How can I make my ex understand that his behaviors are hurting our children?
- How can I get him to follow the parenting plan?
- How can I make him understand that life could be so much better if he would just do what he said that he would do in our divorce decree?
- How can I make him understand?
- Why does he have to be so difficult?

Notice that all of those questions are focused on what you can't control, but in order to create the future you want for you and your children it is imperative you work from where you have control. So what can you control?

The hard truth is that you can only control yourself. You can choose what to think, how to feel, and how to act and react. You and only you. That seems easy to understand but it is not so easy to put into practice. We want the best for our children and we see a clear and logical way to get there. Shouldn't that be what our ex-husband also wants? Perhaps they do and perhaps they don't. What I can tell you is that what they want or think is none of your business. You have to stay out of their business and stay in your own. When you stay in your business, you have some control. When you move into their business, you have no control.

When I found myself trying to change my ex-husband, I was reminded of the powerful words of Bryon Katie, spiritual teacher and author, "There are only three kinds of business in the universe: mine, yours, and God's. Whose business are you in?" When you are in God's business, you are worrying and fretting over what I like to think of as reality. It could be a storm, earthquake, bad traffic, or whether your ex is going to lose his job and stop paying child support. Stop worrying about it. It is something that you have absolutely no control over and agonizing over it is a complete waste of time.

The next is someone else's business and this one is tricky. Every time that we want to control someone's thoughts, words, or actions, we are in their business. I would imagine that you are in someone else's business much of the time. And you probably don't even realize it. We all do it.

- Why does my ex yell at our children all the time?
- Why does he feed our children junk food?
- Why does his girlfriend continue to share her opinions about my children?
- Why does he let our children stay up so late?

Early on, I told my ex how to parent, I told him to follow the parenting plan, I told him what he should and should not be doing. I was way up in his business. And I thought that it was my business. It seemed to be my business. It involved my children and it involved my life so wasn't I supposed to tell him what to do? The truth is that telling him what to do was getting me nowhere and was making my life miserable. Don't get me wrong, my intentions were in the right place but I really had no reason being there. What he did was completely his choice. It was entirely his journey and his path in life and I needed to get out of his way. How arrogant of me to think that I knew what was best for him. How arrogant of me to insert my thoughts and beliefs onto him. He needed to learn some lessons in life and I was interfering with that. This was his life and he would have to reap what he sowed.

Think about your life now. Are you struggling with your ex-husband? Is he making your life and the life of your children difficult?

- Does he show up late for visitation or not even show up?
- Does he miss your child's play, sporting events, or school activities?
- Does he put his own needs and desires in front of your child's?
- Does he continue to disappoint your children and cause them emotional pain?

Can you make him be a better dad? Can you make him be less selfish? Can you make him understand that the choices that he is making are damaging his relationship with his kids?

The answer is NO.

What you can do is be there for your children and support them when they are hurt by their father and offer understanding and love. A word of caution: support and love your child through the disappointments that will come but never badmouth their father. You can criticize his behavior but never him.

Try this, *"I am sorry that your dad did not show up for your play. I know that it hurts when he promised that he would make it."*

The relationship that your child has with his father is their relationship. Whether it is good or bad. You cannot nor should you influence that but be there for them when they are hurt or frustrated. You want to be a source of love and support when they experience sad times in life and you want them to always feel like they can come to you, so remain neutral.

When I really understood this concept and could start to use this in my daily life, it was so liberating. I only had to worry about myself. I only had control over myself. I could really start to imagine a life with my children and stop worrying about how my ex might come in and mess things up. The more that you stay in your own business, the more present you are in your own life. This is the place where change can really occur.

God grant me the serenity to accept the things I cannot change, the courage to change the things I can, and the wisdom to know the difference.

To live the life we want for our future, we have to work with what we can control and one of the things we can control is how we relate to the universe. If we want more peace, joy and ease in our lives, we must change our mindset to make that happen. By focusing on what we can control – how we interact with the world – we can change our lives for ourselves and our children no matter the circumstances. Now is the time to capitalize on the power of intention or what some call, the law of attraction.

So what is the law of attraction? No doubt you have heard this phrase tossed around a lot. And there are many great experts on this topic but what I can offer is an overview of this concept and show you how it has worked in my life and the lives of my clients.

The basic idea of the law of attraction is that everything in the universe is made of energy and energy vibrates. That means that you, me, a tree, and the oceans are all made of energy and we are all vibrating. The idea that we are all energy might sound weird but consider this. How many times have you met someone and immediately felt good? They were emitting a positive, feel good vibration. And on the flip side, how many times have your felt the negative vibe coming off of someone and you just wanted to cut your visit short with them? They were giving off a negative vibration. How about going into someone's home. How did it feel? Positive? Negative? The items in the home are emitting vibrations. And if you stop and think about it, you can feel that energy.

The interesting thing about the law of attraction is that this negative or positive vibration that we are sending out into the world is attracting either negative or positive vibrations. It is the law of physics. Like attracts like. We are really just huge, powerful magnets. Good feelings sync up with good feelings. Bad feelings sync up with bad feelings.

What vibrations are you sending out into the world? Are your feelings filled with worry, gloom and doom? Or are they happy, cheerful, and full of wonder? Worrying is an interesting activity. Worrying really does not get us anywhere but we all do it.

- I worry that my child will become depressed because of the divorce.

- I worry that I will lose my house because I won't be able to make the mortgage payments.
- I worry that my ex will remarry and his new wife will be horrible to my children.
- I worry that the volcano near our home will erupt someday and kill us all.

Does any of this worrying help us? Think of it this way - Worrying is like praying for something to happen. We are placing our attention on what we really don't want instead of what we do want. Try these feel good thoughts instead –

- My child will thrive because of the divorce.
- I love my home and will have the mortgage paid off earlier than I expected.
- My ex will remarry and his new wife will be good to my children.
- The dormant volcano near my home is beautiful and I am blessed to see it every day.

Positive thoughts equal positive vibes being sent out into the world. If you focus upon whatever you want, you will attract that. If you focus upon the *lack* of whatever you want, you will attract more of the lack.

"Our intention creates our reality."
– Wayne Dyer

How do you know for sure what you are focusing on? Here is the trick - check in with how you feel. When you are focusing on what you don't want in your life, you feel bad. You feel exhausted and unmotivated. When you are focusing on what you do want, you feel great! You have energy. It really is the feelings that matter. That is why positive affirmations don't work. I don't care if you spend your entire day saying, "I am happy, I am happy." If you don't feel it, you will not be attracting happiness into your life. The words do not have the same power as the feelings. The feelings in your body are the most important part so be aware of your feelings.

Stop and take inventory of yourself several times a day. Get quiet and observe your thoughts and your feelings. Maybe you have had a particularly bad week with your ex-husband and you are filled with worry and frustration. You feel depleted. Notice it and make an adjustment. Shift your thoughts and then shift your feelings. Get back into your own business; what you can control. Notice beauty around you. Even for a moment. Take a short walk. Notice the beautiful sunny day or the fragrant flowers in your neighbor's yard. Smile at the dog walkers and notice the cute children in strollers. Move into a feeling state of gratitude and joy, if only for a few minutes.

Know that this takes time and practice. You are changing your mindset. You are changing a habit. When things are tough in our lives and one hardship after another comes our way, it is easy to fall into the habit of being "Debbie Downer". And I totally get it. When you are parenting with a difficult ex, life can be one struggle after another. And it can leave you feeling pretty pessimistic. But again, whose business are you in? The question is, "Do want to stay there? Is this a place where you want to be? Or would you rather leave the darkness behind you and come into the light?" The light is where the magic happens. It is where dreams are born. Anything is possible. Come out from under that rock and let your light shine. The world is waiting for you. And so are your children.

Here is a simple formula for you to follow:
- Set your intention.
  » For me it was the future image of my grown daughters, being happy, healthy, and successful young adults
- Envision your dream as if it is already happening.
  » Close your eyes and see it in the future
- Trust that it will happen.
  » Feel the peace in your body of knowing that this will be your reality
- And let it go. Release attachment to the outcome.
  » Don't dwell on it and have grasping energy around it
- Expect the miracle of your vision to become your reality.
  » Know that it will be so and hold onto that vision as your guiding light

This was my vision that I created over 15 years ago and I held it in my mind and believed that it would be my reality. The important thing is that I knew that it would happen and I did not have a doubt in my mind. And with this image permanently residing in my mind, every decision and choice that I made was guided and supported by this picture. And today my daughters are happy, healthy and successful young adults!

A few years after my divorce, I decided that I wanted to go back to work and I knew that I wanted a job that would fit in with my role as a mother. Teaching seemed like a great option. At the same time, my daughters were in elementary school and both were taking Spanish classes. Having lived in Mexico and studied Spanish, I had a lot of opinions about their Spanish instruction. I thought about different ways I could teach and when I was at their school, I told anyone who would listen that I spoke Spanish and loved foreign languages. I also mentioned that I would love to teach Spanish someday. I planted the seed. And then I released attachment to the outcome. One month later, I received a call from the school principal and he told me that the Spanish teacher had quit abruptly and moved back to Chile. They needed a Spanish teacher immediately and my name came up as a possible candidate. Was I interested? Hell yes! I went to school that day and signed a contract to teach Spanish! And here is the interesting thing. At the time, I did not even have a teaching degree. My degree was in business and finance. The law of attraction made it all happen.

I wanted to teach Spanish and I knew that I would someday. I put the request out into the universe and then released attachment to the outcome. When I got that call from the principal and that door opened for me, I walked through it without fear of how I was going to do it. My opportunity appeared and I was going to seize it. I trusted that I would be guided and supported as long as I took the courage to walk through the open door. If I would have been caught up in my ex-husband's business and distracted by him, there wouldn't be a way for me to have taken control of my own destiny. Staying in your own business allows you to be open and aware of all of the possibilities and opportunities that come your way.

Can you remember a time in your life when you wanted something and knew beyond a shadow of a doubt that it would happen? Maybe it was a job, a new home, a car, a vacation destination, or a romantic partner? Think about those times in your life.

- Maybe it was a house that you envisioned and a few years later, you find that you are living in a home just like the one in your dreams.
- Maybe it was a car that you knew that you would be driving someday and a few years later, you own that car.
- Maybe it was a trip to Italy that was always on your mind and several years later, you found yourself sipping wine in Tuscany.
- Maybe it was that wonderful man that came into your life unexpectedly but matched all of the qualities that you were looking for in a partner.

Now apply the law of attraction to your new life as a single parent. What is your vision, your intention for you and your children? Can you see it? Can you feel it? Really breathe that image fully into your mind and body. This is your guiding light.

_____

_____

A client of mine, Ellen, was a skeptic. She was a black and white kinda gal and thought that the law of attraction was quite woo woo. I didn't force the idea on her but asked her to consider making a few small shifts in her life and to see what would happen. What could be the harm? Ellen's world was chaotic since her divorce and she spent much of her time focused on her ex's business and agonized why he didn't spend more time with their children and less time with his girlfriend. She was clearly all up in his business and not focusing on her own. It was time for her to shift her thinking and give the law of attraction a try.

I told her about my daily practice and suggested that she do the same. Every morning before I get out of bed, I take just a few moments to think about my day. I focus on the good things that I want to happen. I imagine it happening and I focus on how I would FEEL when it does happen. *The feelings are more important than the thoughts.* I take a deep breath and really let the image and the feelings expand in my body. Then I get up and start my day. At night I do the same thing. I imagine what I want to have happen in my life. I envision it as if it has already happened and I feel gratitude for it. With that thought in my mind and the good feelings in my body, I close my eyes and go to sleep.

I do add one more activity to my day. I find a time in my day when I can take just five minutes to script about my future self. I write down what I want my life to be as if it is already happening. I cover all topics. Family, finances, work, and health. Whatever comes to me, I just write and don't censor or judge myself. I have fun with it.

Here is an example –

I love my new home. It is so bright and open. Uncluttered and so peaceful. And I love my new neighborhood. My neighbors are so kind and lovely. The dinner party that I attended last night was great. And my ex-husband has been so cooperative lately. My child support payments are always given to me on time and he has stopped arguing with me. What a relief! My new job is amazing. The kids are such a delight and my coworkers are so supportive. I love going to work each day.

This does not take long but it is quite powerful. The important thing to remember is that when you are writing this, you are experiencing the feeling of having all of this in your life already. Don't long for it to happen. It already has. What you really don't want to happen is to be in that grasping energy that we have all felt when we walk into a store and are attacked by the salesperson that wants you desperately to buy something. *Remember that you already have it in your life.*

The energy that you want to feel is peace, love, and gratitude. Believe what you wrote. Know that it is yours and it just has not arrived yet. Again take a deep breath and feel it in your body.

Then shut your journal and go about your day. Do this daily. You will be amazed at the results.

Your thoughts create your world.

Let's go back to Ellen. She told me that she would do these three practices each day for the next 60 days. I wanted her to make this a practice for a couple of months because what she was doing was training her brain to see her world in a new way. She was breaking the habit of being in someone else's business and working on staying in her own. Also she stopped looking at the world in a negative way and replaced it with thoughts of gratitude and possibility.

At the end of the 60 days, Ellen's spirit was lighter and her outlook on life was brighter. The weekly annoyances of her ex did not seem to bother her like they did in the past. And surprisingly his behavior seemed to improve. He paid her child support on time and showed up for visitation when expected. Ellen still wondered how all of this could possibly work but she did not care. She was seeing results in her life and this was something that she was not going to give up.

> *"It is not your work to make anything happen.*
> *It is your work to dream it and let it happen."*
> **– Abraham-Hicks**

Starting a new life for you and your children may seem like a daunting task and I am not going to lie, there is a lot to consider. Before you operated as a family unit and now you are doing it alone. But life is really what you make of it. If you keep wanting things to change that are outside of you or spending too much time ruminating, wondering and worrying because you're involved in other people's business then creating the life you want for you and your children will feel insurmountable. But if you focus on what you can change and your vibration, it will all seem completely possible.

The truth is that we are always getting what we are a vibrational match for, whether we want it or not; it's the law. Remember that we are continually transmitting energy with our thoughts, words, and feelings.

It is important to watch your emotions, your beliefs, and your thoughts. Are your feelings, beliefs, and thoughts negative? Or are they positive? What thoughts are you sending out into the world? What are your thoughts syncing up with? Positive, feel good thoughts or negative, feel bad thoughts? Remember if you are sending negative thoughts out into the world, you are attracting negative things into your life. When life is difficult, negative thoughts are natural. Thoughts of worry or despair are common. Even when you are basically a positive person, it becomes so easy to fall into the trap of worrying about everything around you and by the way everything that you really have no control over. The first step is to recognize this. The next step is to find some positive images, and start to get those positive feelings to flow. Start small but please do start.

Begin with taking 10 minutes a day to notice the good things in your life. It might look like this –

- My home is beautiful

- I have a sweet and kind neighbor
- My children are healthy
- My ex was kind to me today
- I have a loving and supportive family
- The meal that I made today was delicious
- I love my new haircut

Start to send out feel good vibrations into the world, even if it is just for 10 minutes a day. You will begin to feel the shift occurring in you.

When you are trying to co-parent with an uncooperative ex, it might be hard to find those positive feelings and break the habit of worrying. But it is well worth the effort. You will begin to shift from feelings of worry and anxiety to feelings of joy and ease. You will start to journey down a new path and doors will begin to open for you. When the doors open, have the courage to walk through them. What is on the other side is something that you could not even imagine. Dwell in a place of wonder and possibility, not a place of fear and limitations.

"There are only two ways to live your life. One is as though nothing is a miracle.
The other is as though everything is a miracle."
– Albert Einstein

CHAPTER 6

Take Action

"You don't have to see the whole staircase,
just take the first step."
- Martin Luther King, Jr.

Most of us expect our lives after divorce to be irrevocably changed and we try to prepare ourselves for that transition. There are added responsibilities and new roles to fill. It is an unsettling time that can leave us feeling lost and confused. When we find ourselves co-parenting with an uncooperative ex, the stress of post-divorce life reaches an all-time high. There always seems to be so much to do and every time we feel like we are getting ahead, our ex comes in and hijacks our progress and our energy. He can steal away our peace of mind, our time, and our finances. How do we handle it all without being totally stressed out?

It begins with small but consistent steps in the direction of our goals. We need to commit to making a plan to move forward despite the chaos. When we take action toward what we want we spend more time cultivating the life we want for our children and ourselves and less time overwhelmed with what our ex isn't or shouldn't be doing.

Movement is the key. It is magical. Doors will open for you and opportunities will appear. It can be very scary to take that first step or even that hundredth step, but that is where your life really begins. In this chapter I'm going to show you different ways you can take action now.

Visualize

Visualize some areas in your life where you would like to accomplish personal or professional goals. Or maybe something new for your home or family. Would you like to make some new friends? Start a new career? Look for a new home? Reconnect with your extended family? Focus on one goal and decide that you will create some movement today toward that objective. One of the easiest ways to do that is to break down your task into ridiculously small steps. And then feel the sense of accomplishment that you did what you planned to do.

What about some of your goals or dreams that are more long term? What is the best way to start moving toward making them a reality? A really helpful way to reach them is to work backwards. Most of us look at our goals and just start heading in that direction with the hope that we will someday get there.

And you might get there but working backwards seems to be the golden ticket.

Close your eyes and picture yourself one year from now. Use the law of attraction techniques that you learned from the last chapter. Really feel it in your body. Believe that you can achieve this image of you in the future. Where do you live? What do you look like? What are you wearing? Where are you working? What school are your children attending? Stay with this image for a few minutes. Take a deep breath and believe that you have it already. Open your eyes, write it down, and get started on making it your reality.

My life, one year from today -

_____

_____

_____

_____

_____

_____

_____

_____

_____

_____

This was one of my images that I wanted to make into a reality when I was newly divorced. I wanted to have a mind and body that was strong and healthy. I knew that single parenting was going to be exhausting and I wanted to be in excellent shape. And of course, I also wanted to feel good about myself.

The first step toward that goal was to make a plan to incorporate exercise into my life. Back then I was working with a coach and she suggested that I work backwards. I imagined my future self, strong both mentally and physically. I loved that image. Now I needed to make it a reality. Money was tight so I needed to find something that worked with my schedule and my budget. I did some research and talked to people and I found a community center that was affordable and had a great schedule of activities. I made a commitment to add this to my life and by the end of the year, my image had become a reality. It was a small step but it was movement. And that small step created big results in twelve months.

How about you? Do you have an image of yourself twelve months from now? Are you in a new home or in a new job? Make that image your guiding light and begin to work backwards. Get out a calendar and fill in each month the little steps that you can take to make that image a reality. And break your tasks down into incredibly small steps.

My client, Liz, had alimony for three years but wondered what she would like to do after that time. We talked about career possibilities. I asked Liz to list several jobs that were attractive to her and to imagine doing that work. All aspects of the job. As Liz imagined her new career possibilities, I told her to close her eyes and see if her body was sending her any messages about any of them. It became very clear to Liz that the one that really made her feel joyful was nursing. This was perfect because Liz discovered that she would have to go to school for three years which was the exact time frame that she would have the financial freedom to do so. Liz left that day with just a few small tasks to accomplish and we decided to check in the following week to see her progress. She continued to take one small step at a time and chose not to become overwhelmed by the process. Before long, Liz was enrolled in nursing school and had a graduation date three months before her alimony ended. She thought about her future self and worked backwards in order to make her dream a reality.

As you move through your list of goals and responsibilities, make sure that you don't fall into the trap of trying to do everything perfectly. This is a familiar place for me. I like to see myself, as a recovering perfectionist but the truth is that I do suffer from relapses. I used to feel like I needed to do everything perfectly. I had to be the perfect mom, the perfect daughter, and the perfect ex-wife. I wouldn't allow any mistakes to be made. That was a tremendous pressure that I placed on myself. Perfection is not reality. Who really is perfect? Not one of us. And who defines perfection? It is best that you give up the idea of being perfect. Be real. Be human. And remember, done is better than perfect.

Create a To Do List

To-do-lists can be a great way to stay organized and take action but they can also cause paralysis. The best thing you can do is to take some control of your list. Do you really need to be worrying about everything that is on your list right now? Surely all of it does not need to be accomplished today. Separate the list into short term and long-term tasks. That should cut it in half. Next pull out the urgent ones that need to be focused on today. Finally, take a look and notice if you have written that you *HAVE* to do something.

- *I have to* make cupcakes for my daughter's school.
- *I have to* return my ex-husband's phone call.

Do you really have to? Couldn't you just buy cupcakes at the store? Couldn't you respond to your ex-husband via email? Or not respond at all?

Stop doing what you *HAVE* to do and change it to *I CHOOSE* to do. Don't be held hostage by your to-do-list. You are in charge so start choosing to do what you want to do. The energetic shift of using these two words, *I CHOOSE* is incredible. Start choosing what you want to do right now.

Some days you feel great and think you can accomplish anything but also be prepared for those other days where you might feel completely overwhelmed and feel like you can't get off of the couch. I have experienced them and so have my clients. When I feel completely stuck and cannot move in any direction, I imagine my mind as a computer and I realize that I have too many tabs open. My computer begins to run slowly and is completely inefficient. Everything that I try to do seems to take longer than necessary. I become discouraged and eventually take to the couch with a bag of cookies. The computer screen in my head is frozen and locked up. What can I do? What would you do with your computer?

- Shut it all down.
- Close all of the tabs.

- Breathe. Deeply.
- Put the cookies down.
- Move around. Go for a walk or at the very least step outside and breathe some fresh air. Give yourself some compassion and love.
- Now reboot.
- Open just one tab and focus on that task.
- And when that job is completed, open the next tab.
- Work on that and when it is finished, close it.
- Move through your tabs just one at a time.

We cannot progress when we are stressed out or when we force something. We will get so much more done through ease and flow and not through panic and force. Swimming upstream is exhausting. How about turning yourself around and start going with the flow?

When you check something off of your list, take a moment to acknowledge that it is completed. Give yourself one small goal today that you think you can accomplish. Open a new bank account, join a gym, meet someone for lunch and start to network. Don't make it too big, just something that you'll look back on in the future and feel good.

Set Boundaries

After her divorce was final, Karen hoped that co-parenting with her ex would not be too difficult. She tried to maintain peace by allowing her ex to stop by her home and to call her and the children whenever he wanted. What started out as a friendly gesture on her part, soon turned into a situation that resembled a marriage. Her ex seemed to be at her home more than his own. The new life that Karen had envisioned for her and her children was not happening. Not even close. Karen knew that she had to establish boundaries when it came to her home and her sanity. She felt uncomfortable doing this but knew that in the long run, it would pay off. Her ex did not like it at first but Karen did not give in to his tantrums. She was uneasy about taking this step but she found out that doing so actually gave her strength. When you start to speak your truth and make your desires known, you will find more courage than you thought you ever had.

Here are some of the boundaries that my clients have used to help them move forward after divorce. Maybe some of these may be helpful for you.

- Minimize contact with your ex and set boundaries about communication. Email rather than communicate over the phone or in person. It takes the emotion out of it and gives you time to think about what you want to say. Also, just stick to the facts in communication. If your ex is a narcissist, they love to get you riled up so don't give into them. An added bonus is that you will have everything in writing.

- When you do see your ex, vow to be calm, cool, and collected. They really do love to shake you up so that they can then tell everyone that you are unstable. Do not give them any ammunition. They also like to keep you drawn into the relationship and engaged in psychological battles. Decline the invitation!

- Keep your home, your home. You might need to remind your ex that this is your home and not a place for him to visit with the children.

I believe that whatever journey you are on, how difficult it is has a lot to do with attitude. I am not minimizing how hard the struggles can be when you find yourself in a post-divorce combat zone but what I am saying is that you get to decide your attitude. Are you going to face your day with purpose and conviction or with confusion and doubt? Look at every day as a new opportunity to move towards something wonderful and leave the past behind you. Tomorrow is gone and truly the future is uncertain but what you really have is today. Make it great. Continue to take small steps in the direction of your new life. Each time you challenge yourself, you gain confidence and strength and the ability to take the next step.

CHAPTER 7

Be Your Own Hero

"Above all, be the heroine of your life,
not the victim."
— **Nora Ephron**

imagine when you began your journey through the legal system with your divorce you had faith in the courts, the judges, and the lawyers. You believed that if you did the right thing and if you followed the rules, all would be well. I suspect that you held this belief because I am quite familiar with it as well. That was my fantasy. I had this naive notion that everyone could see that I had the best interest of my children as my primary focus. I became saddened and disillusioned by what I experienced. It was not that the courts, judges or lawyers were not competent or compassionate, but what I came to realize was

73

that they could only do so much. The rest was up to me. I had to step up to the plate and take charge of my life and the lives of my daughters. God helps those who help themselves and I knew that I needed to grab onto the reigns and take control.

Perhaps you are feeling the same way as I did many years ago. If so, then it is critical for you to be your own champion and for you to make things happen in your life. You become your own advocate by not looking back, asking for help, having faith, taking care of yourself, learning lessons, getting back up, and finding your strength.

Stop Looking Back

You may wonder, how did I get here? That is a good question and perhaps it might be a good topic to discuss with a therapist. I know that was a question that my mom continued to ask me until I politely told her that a more important question was, "What the hell am I going to do now?" I chose to stop looking back and focus my attention on the present and future.

One of my clients, Stella, was notorious for spending her time brooding about the past. "Why was my ex so mean to me? Why did I marry him? Why did I stay married for so long?" So many questions that kept holding her back and preventing her from moving forward. Decide today that you are going to write a new chapter in your life and move forward and not get stuck in the stories of the past. When I was faced with divorce followed by years of stressful co-parenting, I had to figure out how to survive and create a peaceful life for my daughters and myself. I knew that creating a life of joy and ease meant I had to leave the past behind because if I stayed there, I was going to continue to get the same results.

By looking forward and knowing what you want your future to be you're in a better position to make strides toward making it happen. Being your own advocate means letting go of the past in order to make decisions for your future.

Ask for Help

During my divorce and the early years that followed I realized that I could not do it all on my own. I am very independent and was accustomed to not asking for help. But my experience forced me to see that asking for help and having a supportive community was actually helping me be an advocate for my future. Without the help of others, I wouldn't have been able to keep up with my children's activities or my home.

Why was I so reluctant to let others pitch in? Part of it is the American way. We are so independent and proud and love to announce to everyone, "I am strong, I can do it all on my own!" We feel ashamed to ask for help.

Sue had been a stay at home mom for many years and after her divorce she went back into the workforce. She had a flexible workweek but it was still quite an adjustment for her and her sons. At first, Sue still tried to pick the boys up from school and take them to all of their activities and then come home and cook a nutritious dinner. She was wearing herself out and the stress of trying to do it all was creating tension in her home. She hated that she snapped at her children and that she was always on edge but Sue was reluctant to ask for help. She was used to doing it all on her own. When Sue and I spoke, we looked at her schedule and her commitments. What she was trying to do was not sustainable and she knew that she had to make a change and ask for help both from her children and her friends. Sue asked other parents to carpool with her to activities and asked her sons to help out more around the house. When she did this, she discovered a wonderful community of parents that were not only willing to help but wanted to help.

Faith

I could not have weathered this storm without my faith. When I really opened that pathway between God and me, the whispers of love and support came flooding in. I remember one afternoon that I went to mass after having a big disappointment in court. I knelt down and began to pray for courage and strength to keep going. I was disillusioned and unsure what to do next. When I stopped praying, I looked up and next to me was a station of the cross image. It said, "Jesus falls down and someone from the crowd helps him to carry his cross." I felt like that message was placed there for me personally. It gave me the strength to move forward and continue to fight for my children. A peace came over me and I knew that I would be supported that day and every day forward.

As you move through this tough journey of co-parenting, messages of hope and clarity will pop into your head, be on a billboard or be spoken by a stranger. Think back to your journey and look for those guides that have been placed in your path. They have always been there, but maybe you were too busy to notice. Commit to being open to the magical support that will come your way. Sometimes all it takes is awareness and trust.

Take Care of Yourself

Your journey with an ex that fights you every step of the way is long and draining. So taking care of you is critical. And that means physically, spiritually, and emotionally. Consider joining a single parenting group. Or work with a therapist or a life coach. Look for ways to fill up your tank because you can't run on empty for too long.

Add self-care to your daily routine, even if it is for only a few minutes a day. Consider waking up 30 minutes earlier and taking that peaceful, quiet time in the morning for you. Think about the day ahead and look back and notice how much you really have accomplished. Give yourself a pat on the back. You really do need to be your biggest fan and not your worst critic. Make that shift not just for yourself but for your kids as well. They need the best version of you. And you can give it to them.

Sometimes self-care is just collapsing on the couch after the kids leave for visitation with their father. I remember when my daughters went for the weekend to see their dad. I was so mentally, emotionally, and physically exhausted by the time that they left, that all I could do was lie down and begin a *Law & Order* marathon. I am a very high-energy person but I literally could not move for hours and I felt guilty about it. Surely there were things that I needed to do. Clean the house, do the laundry, or go to the grocery store. Thank God that my brilliant counselor told me to lighten up and just surrender to my body and what it needed. My tank was depleted and I needed to refuel.

What is your favorite method to refill your tank? Long walks in nature? Going to the gym? Visiting with friends?

Watching a whole Netflix series in one weekend? You must give yourself what you need to get the strength and energy to face your next hurdle.

Learn Your Lesson

This is not happening to you –
It is happening for you. Your soul is on a journey.

As you move forward with your new life, you might notice that a familiar struggle keeps showing up. Maybe it is establishing boundaries with others. Maybe it is speaking up for yourself and not worrying about whose feelings you might hurt. If you've ever asked yourself this question, "Why is this happening to me?" you are not alone. One of the first self-help books that I read many years ago was *The Seat of the Soul* by Gary Zukav. It was one of those really dense and powerful books that change your perspective but it takes time. At least it did for me. I would read one paragraph, put the book down, and think about it for a few days. And then I would read another paragraph and ponder it for a while. Needless to say, the book took a long time to digest but it was well worth it. It helped me to understand why some struggles continued to appear in my life. Until you learn your lesson in the Earth School, the universe will continue to send you similar situations from which you can grow and learn. You can't skip the lesson. You can't avoid it. It will continue to appear.

What was one of my lessons? Stay in my own truth and set strong and clear boundaries with others. And be unapologetic about it! It took me awhile to learn this lesson, but I did. I had to!

Think about it. What challenges keep showing up in your life? Same problem, different people, different situation? Can you see a pattern? This is a growth opportunity for you. It won't be easy because if it were, you would have mastered it already. Once you learned that lesson, there will be more to follow for your soul's journey. Reframe your struggles as growth opportunities. So when your ex continues to cross boundaries and disrespect you, approach it as a growth opportunity. This is a great time for you to really make some big changes in your life. A time for creating a world where you are growing and changing and continuing to evolve into a better version of yourself. One day at a time. One lesson at a time.

"Every moment is an invitation to live out of your
weakness or to live out of your strength."
- Marianne Williamson

Get Back Up

Being the hero of your own story takes grit. Some days will be easier than others but remember to move forward and to get back on your feet no matter how many times you fall. Your children are watching you and you are modeling for them how to deal with difficult people and situations. Don't you want your child to grow up as a strong and resourceful person and not have a victim mentality? Talk to your child and more importantly *listen.* They will need to process all that they have witnessed and it might also be wise to find them their own personal counselor. The time and money that you put into your kids early on will pay off in the long run. Don't wait for them to be adults before they begin to sort all of this out. Start now and empower your child to use their voice and learn to set their own boundaries.

Find Your Strength

Know where you can find your strength. Is it in the gym? Is it in the church? Is it through meditation? Is it through your family? Your friends? Be familiar with it and go to that place for strength because you are going to need it.

For me, I imagined my ancestors in Ireland, living on a farm during the famine years. We still have that farm and I have walked those fields and envisioned their life 150 years ago. How did they survive? Where did they find the strength? Surely they were very strong and resourceful.

When things became particularly chaotic in my life, I closed my eyes and thought about my ancestors. I knew that the strength they must have carried with them also resides in my DNA. I knew that I could survive this time in my life and not only that, I knew that I could thrive and so could my children. I closed my eyes and thought of them and asked them for wisdom, strength and courage. I thought, *Hell, if they could survive the famine, then I could certainly survive this!*

Who can you call upon? Someone who is alive and in your life now? Or someone from the spiritual world? How about both? What is your ancestor's story? I am sure that they endured much and can offer both inspiration and love. Ask for it. Wait.

Ask again. Breathe. Trust that they are there and always wanting the best for you.

Being a single parent is a tough job especially when you find yourself battling with a difficult ex. It can take all of your strength, creativity, and perseverance. Along the way, it will be imperative that you speak up for yourself. You cannot afford to wait for others to save you and your children, you have to save yourself and be your own advocate. If you don't, who will?

CHAPTER 8

My Wish for You

"My mission in life is not merely to survive, but to thrive; And to do so with some passion, some compassion, some humor, and some style."
- Maya Angelou

Right now, you might be where I was many years ago, in the fog of constant stress and conflict with your ex. You might feel overwhelmed and distracted by the worry and anxiety of how this is affecting your children. And you might not be able to see clearly how you can move through this. But I can see it. Your life on the other side of darkness awaits you. I know that you can get there and when you do, you too will be a stronger, wiser, and more confident woman and mother.

I have worked with many women that are just like you. Newly divorced and ready to create a new life but find that their ex continues to create roadblocks at every turn. It is exhausting and it leaves little time for you to plan for your future. I've worked with these women to help them look at their current situation and craft a plan to help them move from a place of despair to a place of hope and possibility.

My client, Rita, has made some incredible changes in her life in the past year. When she and I first began working together, she was completely exhausted and full of anger. Her ex had filled her life with constant drama, conflict, and court appearances. Not a week went by that her ex did not do something to her – name-calling, yelling, or threatening to take her to court. Each time that would happen, Rita reacted with anger and fear and felt like she was perpetually in the state of fight or flight. Her immune system was taking a beating from this and she was sick all the time. Rita felt like she was caught in a roundabout and could not see a way to exit. Her natural instinct was to be protective of her children and to fight for what she believed was right but all of this arguing was not helping her to move forward.

We talked about what she would like her life to look like. I asked her if she could let go of the anger, resentment, and the need for revenge. I told her that the best revenge is to live a fabulous life.

Rita was ready to make some changes. She knew that she could not continue living the way she had been. After working together three months, she made some huge shifts in her mindset that translated to even bigger shifts in her life. She first was able to get to a place of greater clarity and see that what she had been doing was not really helping her achieve any real peace in her life. Next she learned to trust her own intuition and got in touch with her internal wisdom and began to trust herself as the expert in her life. Finally, Rita started to dream of a new life for her and her children and used the power of intention to help make it a reality.

I can tell you that today she is the opposite of the woman I met a year ago. Rita has taken back her power and this has spilled over into other aspects of her life. She now has a vision for her future and a plan of how to get there. Her home is calmer and she has more energy and patience for her children. She also is exploring new career opportunities and is planning a move. The weekly struggles with her ex are less frequent and they certainly don't derail her like they once did in the past.

More importantly, she no longer grabs the rope when her ex dangles it in front of her. He's lost his power and control. She gained her sanity and sense of joy. Sure there are still some fires that need to be put out from time to time but the intensity of the flame has decreased. And Rita now has the knowledge of how to use the extinguisher to put it out.

When your ex finally understands that you are no longer a willing participant in his games, it is not fun any longer for him. He usually will look for someone else to play. Either way, you will be focused less on him and more on you and your children. Your focus will be right where it needs to be – creating a fabulous life for you and your children! Sometimes just making one small shift in your mindset will create a rippling effect in your entire life.

My wish for you is that this book will be that light to help you see through the darkness. Through my story and those of my clients, I hope that you gain inspiration, hope, and some great tools to help you get to a place of peace, confidence and strength. Life can be wonderful on the other side of divorce with a difficult ex. A life filled with laughter and joy. It can happen.

ACKNOWLEDGEMENTS

This book has been a long time in the making. So many of my friends and family told me for years to write a book and without their love and support it would not have become a reality.

I must also thank my mother, who has always been there right beside me offering encouragement and incredible insight. How did I ever get so lucky to call you mom?

And to my father, my guiding light and the very best role model that any child could ever have had. There is not a day that goes by that I do not think of you and your wisdom, stories, and great wit. Each day with you was a blessing and even though you are no longer with me physically, I feel your presence.

Erin and Máire, you have blessed my life with more love, laughter, and adventure than I imagined possible and you inspire me daily. Being your mother is my greatest joy.

I am grateful to Bob and Ellen for their support and encouragement over the years. You have always been a source of strength for me.

Thank you Connie, my partner in crime and fellow dreamer. I deeply appreciate your friendship and our marathon phone calls.

Thank you Jim for encouraging me to keep writing even when I desperately wanted to be distracted. You helped me keep my eye on the prize.

Thank you Susan Austin-Crumpton who started me on this journey of awakening and always challenged me to be my very best.

To my fabulous legal team that became my friends, Greg Smith, Joanna Montgomery, and Jim Martin, your expertise and support throughout the years have been a precious gift to my girls and me.

To my wonderful clients who have trusted me with their stories and allowed me to guide them through their journeys. It has been an honor to be your coach.

Finally, this book would not be here today without the help and guidance of Cynthia Kane and Angela Lauria. Thank you Cynthia for keeping me on track and encouraging me to keep going! Thank you Angela for your coaching and wisdom. I am so very grateful that you helped me take my book from an idea to a finished product and for the powerful transformation that I experienced along the way.

ABOUT THE AUTHOR

Maureen is a coach, international best-selling author, teacher, and speaker, with proven expertise in the divorce recovery field. Combining straight talk, empathy and laughter, she helps her clients rebuild their lives after divorce and raise healthy, happy children.

Maureen studied at The Martha Beck Institute and received her Bachelor of Science from DePaul University and her Master of Art in Teaching from Trevecca Nazarene University.

She lives in Nashville and is successfully navigating her way through single life. Maureen is proud to have co-parented her two daughters who are thriving in their early 20's and enjoys traveling, reading, and checking out the newest restaurants with friends.

Website: http://maureen-doyle.com

Email: Maureen@maureen-doyle.com

THANK YOU

Thank you for reading *When Your Ex Doesn't Follow The Rules!* This isn't the end but rather the beginning of creating a peaceful future for you and your children.

Keep the momentum going! To support you in your journey of co-parenting, I created a **Co-Parenting Survival Kit** just for you.

Co-Parenting Survival Kit includes:

- How to Get Your Ex to Follow the Rules Checklist
- Quick Reference Guide for High Stress Encounters with Your Ex
- Worksheets to accompany the exercises from this book

You can access this kit at:
www.whenyourexdoesntfollowtherulesbook.com

If you would like to speak to me personally about your co-parenting journey, let's have a conversation. You can schedule your complimentary conversation at www.talktomaureen.com.

Morgan James
Speakers Group

www.TheMorganJamesSpeakersGroup.com

We connect Morgan James published
authors with live and online events
and audiences whom will benefit
from their expertise.

CPSIA information can be obtained
at www.ICGtesting.com
Printed in the USA
BVOW03s0546240817
492968BV00001B/3/P